Daily Life in THE ISLAMIC GOLDEN AGE

Don Nardo

heinemann raintree

© 2015 Heinemann Raintree
an imprint of Capstone Global Library, LLC
Chicago, Illinois

To contact Capstone Global Library, please call 800-747-4992, or visit our web site www.capstonepub.com

Edited by Clare Lewis and Catherine Neitge
Designed by Philippa Jenkins
Original illustrations © Capstone Global Library Limited 2015
Illustrated by HL Studios, Witney, Oxon
Picture research by Jo Miller
Production by Helen McCreath
Originated by Capstone Global Library Ltd
Printed and bound in China by CTPS

18 17 16 15 14
10 9 8 7 6 5 4 3 2 1

Library of Congress Cataloging-in-Publication Data
Nardo, Don, 1947-
  Daily life in the Islamic Golden Age / Don Nardo.
    pages cm.—(Daily life in ancient civilizations)
  Includes bibliographical references and index.
  ISBN 978-1-4846-0831-9 (hb)—ISBN 978-1-4846-0836-4 (pb)—ISBN 978-1-4846-0846-3 (ebook) 1. Islamic Empire—History—Juvenile literature. 2. Islam—History—Juvenile literature I. Title.

  DS37.7.N365 2015
  909'.0976701—dc23   2014029726

This book has been officially leveled by using the F&P Text Level Gradient™ Leveling System.

Acknowledgments
We would like to thank the following for permission to reproduce photographs:Alamy: Art Directors & TRIP/ArkReligion.com, 8, David South, 9, Finnbar, 7, Images & Stories, 10, incamerastock, 13 (top), Karol Kozlowski, 27, Lanmas, 14, LatitudeStock/Allan Hartley, 13 (bottom), North Wind Picture Archive, 38, Oldtime, 24; Bridgeman Art Library: Bibliotheque Nationale, Paris, France/Giraudon, 35, British Library, London UK, 16, Christie's Images/Private Collection, 28, Egyptian National Library, Cairo, Egypt, 31, Museum of the Holy Ma'sumeh Shrine, Qom, Iran, 37, Universal History Archive/UIG, 33; Glow Images: GraphEast/Dominic Byrne, 22; Newscom: akg-images, 5, 39, akg-images/Bildarchiv Steffens, 6, akg-images/Philippe Maillard, 15, Universal Images Group/Leemage, 20, VWPics/Mel Longhurst, 23, 34, 36; Photoshot: Quint Lox, 42; Science Source: Jessica Wilson, 25; Shutterstock: ILeysen, 41, M R, 41; SuperStock: age fotostock, cover, Universal Images Group, 30; Wikipedia, 18
Design Elements: Nova Development Corporation, clip art (throughout), Shutterstock: imanolqs

We would like to thank Professor Timothy Insoll for his invaluable help in the preparation of this book.

CONTENTS

Some words are shown in bold, **like this**. You can find out what they mean by looking in the glossary.

In 750 **CE**, a ruler named Abu al-Abbas al-Saffah came to power in a mighty empire. It stretched from Afghanistan in the east to Morocco in the west. Al-Saffah was given the title **caliph**, which meant leader of the **Muslim** community. Muslims were followers of the religion known as **Islam**, just as they are today.

The will of Allah

In religious matters, al-Saffah and other Muslims of his day had a strong role model. He was Islam's founder, the **prophet** Muhammad. Born in Mecca, in western Arabia, in about 570 CE, the prophet Muhammad worked as a merchant in his early adult years. He said that when he was around 40 years old, the angel Gabriel appeared to him.

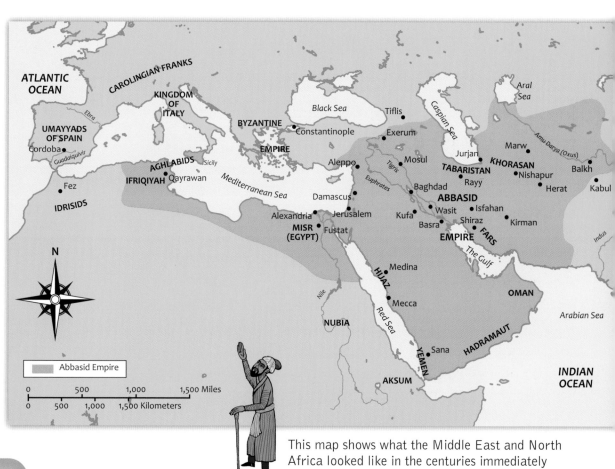

This map shows what the Middle East and North Africa looked like in the centuries immediately following the Arab Muslims' takeover of that region.

This artist's impression shows Baghdad during the Islamic Golden Age—a bustling, vibrant city.

The heavenly angel said that God had chosen Muhammad as his prophet, meaning his messenger. The prophet Muhammad's task as messenger would be to reveal God's will to humans. He taught that there is only one god, whose Arabic name is **Allah**.

The prophet Muhammad steadily gathered **converts** to a new religion called Islam. By the time he died in 632 CE, there were many thousands of Muslims in Arabia. Muslims soon conquered all of the **Middle East** and then swept across North Africa. These Muslims usually did not force the defeated people to convert to Islam, but eventually most of them did so on their own.

A new dynasty

In 750 CE, there was no way to know that al-Saffah's family—the Abbasids—would rule for around 500 years. During the first 300 years of their rule, the Abbasid caliphs would oversee great advances in the arts, literature, and science. Today, it is seen as one of history's most splendid cultural golden ages.

For early Muslims, including those of the Golden Age, the **rituals** of their religion were central to their daily lives. Saying daily prayers was only one of several religious rituals begun earlier by the prophet Muhammad. All Muslims followed these rituals.

This colorful picture from a 16th-century Turkish manuscript shows the angel Gabriel grasping the prophet Muhammad's hand.

A book central to people's lives

The rituals in question were all laid out in Islam's holy book, the Quran. This special book also contains a number of rules. Some are guidelines for Muslims' daily lives. Others are instructions for how to build and maintain a fair society.

THE FINAL PROPHET

One major idea in the Quran is that only one god exists. Another is that the prophet Muhammad was God's final prophet. God had chosen other prophets before. Among them were Abraham, Moses, and Jesus, men highly respected by Jews and Christians. Muslims therefore believe that all three faiths worship the same god. In fact, Islam calls members of these religions the "people of the book." For Jews, that "book" is the Old Testament. For Christians, it is the New Testament. And for Muslims, it is the Quran.

A copy of Islam's most sacred and respected book, the Quran, rests on a Muslim prayer rug.

The ritual of prayer

The Quran lists five main rituals of worship. They are often called Islam's Five Pillars. The first pillar, recognized by Golden Age and modern Muslims alike, is a basic statement of belief. Called the *shahadah*, it says that there is no other god but Allah, and that the prophet Muhammad is his messenger. Muslims can say it at any time. But usually they say it during prayer.

Muslims today still pray to God five times a day.

Daily prayer itself, called salah, is Islam's second pillar. As they do today, during the Golden Age, Muslims prayed to Allah five times each day. Sometimes they prayed in an Islamic place of worship, called a mosque. They could also pray at home or at work. Usually they first crossed their arms across their chests and spoke some verses from the Quran. Then they dropped to their knees and repeated a few more verses.

The worshipper always faced in a certain direction while praying. The prophet Muhammad said that the faithful should pray toward Mecca. The reason was that an extremely sacred structure stood in that city. It was called the Kaaba. The early Muslims believed that the first version of the Kaaba had been built long ago by the prophet Abraham and his son, Ishmael.

Muezzins still call the faithful to prayer in Muslim communities all over the world.

THE ROLE OF THE MUEZZIN

An important tradition related to salah is calling the faithful to prayer five times a day. In the Golden Age, just like today, an official at a local mosque delivered this reminder. He was called a muezzin. He traditionally gave the call in Arabic and in musical tones.

The Kaaba in Mecca is visited by hundreds of thousands of Muslims every year.

The other pillars of worship

Fulfilling the last three of Islam's pillars was also important in the lives of Golden Age Muslims. The third pillar, called *zakat*, consists of giving charity to the poor. In Abbasid times, as today, all Muslims who had enough money to do so were expected to help those less fortunate than themselves. Such giving could happen daily, monthly, or any time during the year the giver was able. The belief was that if people with the means to give refused, God would eventually punish them.

The fourth pillar, which most Golden Age Muslims closely observed, is called *sawm*. It means fasting, or temporarily giving up eating and drinking. To observe *sawm*, most Muslims did not eat or drink from sunrise to sunset during the holy month of Ramadan. (The exact dates for Ramadan vary from year to year.) It was believed that such fasting gave thanks to Allah for his many blessings.

The last of the five pillars is called the **Hajj**. It consists of making a **pilgrimage** to Mecca at least once in a person's lifetime. Ever since the prophet Muhammad's time, every Muslim who was physically able to fulfilled this duty. When that person arrived in Mecca, he or she walked seven times around the sacred Kaaba. The person also took part in other local religious activities.

THE SACRED KAABA

The Kaaba is a cube-shaped stone building about 43 feet (13 meters) tall and a bit less than that wide. There is a sacred black rock inside it. According to tradition, the rock fell from heaven long ago. Muslims believe that the spot where it landed was where God wanted the first humans, Adam and Eve, to put up an altar.

The types of houses people lived in during Islam's Golden Age varied considerably. Homes in the countryside usually differed in design and materials from those in the cities.

Nomads and poorer people

Many people during the Abbasid centuries were **nomads**. They were people without permanent homes. Instead, they wandered through the countryside, making their livings by herding animals.

The most common nomads in the Middle East were Arab Bedouins. Generally, they lived in tents that they could quickly put up and take down, though they sometimes built simple huts. The tents were made from either goat or camel hair or leather made from camel hide.

HOW DO WE KNOW?

City housing

Cities during the Golden Age had both single homes and multistory buildings that often housed more than one family. The most important Abbasid city was Baghdad, in central Iraq. Its biggest single homes were the rulers' palaces. Made of stone and brick, they had many rooms. Some also had small zoos and very large gardens. The average single city home had several rooms, arranged around a central courtyard. The larger buildings often stood four or five stories high. Made from stone, brick, and timber, each could hold up to 200 people. Quite a bit is known about housing in Baghdad and other Abbasid towns. Excavations at Samarra in 1936-1939 revealed part of a palace and the foundations of several houses.

Most homes in the countryside were the one-room shacks of poor farmers. Like the small huts the nomads built, these shacks had dirt floors. It was common for the farmers to share their small living spaces with their sheep and other animals.

Permanent homes

Better-off country dwellers, including a few nomads and some farmers, could afford more permanent houses called *qasr*. These were larger homes made of stone or brick. For both privacy and protection, they were surrounded by high walls. These walls held storerooms for food and stalls and pens for donkeys and other animals. Often there was also a well to provide water.

The ruins of this castle fortress can be found in Jordan. They date from the 8th century.

The Qasr Kharanah is a desert castle and is one of the earliest surviving examples of Islamic architecture. Experts believe it was built in the 8th century CE.

Furniture and Lighting

The furniture of homes during the Abbasid period varied according to the family's wealth. The furnishings of ordinary homes were simple. Average city dwellers included craftworkers, shopkeepers, and merchants who sold their wares in open-air marketplaces. These workers and their families slept on mattresses on the floor. They also sat on low sofas and large pillows. Dining tables were close to the floor, too, so it was common to sit on the floor while eating.

Richer city dwellers included doctors, government officials, and army officers. They could afford beds with modern-style wooden frames and chairs with legs like those used today. They could also afford to cover some of their floors with expensive carpets.

Mats made of reeds made sitting on the floor more comfortable and protected the beautiful carpets.

Another common home furnishing was seen in both rich and average homes. It consisted of devices to keep a house cool in hot weather. These were typically grills or screens made of strips of wood that formed complex patterns. As window coverings, these screens reduced incoming sunlight, yet allowed breezes to filter through. They also provided some privacy.

Interior lighting after sunset came from oil lamps and candles. The lamps were most often made of baked clay. They burned olive oil and animal fat.

This mosque lamp is made from copper and would have burned oil.

HOW DO WE KNOW?

Finely made carpets

The furnishings of wealthy homes and the palaces of the Abbasid rulers included expensive carpets. Many were of Persian design and made in what is now Iran. Others came from North Africa. They are described in writings of the Abbasid period. But only a few of these rugs have survived. The Asian Art Museum in San Francisco, California, has a carpet that may date to the Abbasid period. Now worn and frayed, it features the image of a lion.

Common foods and drinks

In an average Golden Age house, meals were prepared in the kitchen, often located in part of the courtyard. Usually there was a charcoal-burning oven. It was shaped like a big pot with its bottom-side up. The cook—usually one of the women in the family—placed the items to be baked inside through an opening in the side. Also common to Golden Age kitchens was a brick or stone fireplace that could hold several pots at once. The pots were made of copper, fired clay, and sometimes iron.

Wealthy people could afford the most expensive foods. Here, a nobleman feasts with his guests in one of his mansion's courtyards.

Bread was usually made from wheat or barley. Rice was available in some areas. And olives and grapes came from orchards and vineyards along the Mediterranean coasts. Other common fruits included dates, watermelons, and mangoes. For meat, people ate lamb, poultry, camel meat, beef, and fish. Among the dairy products, which came from goats and other livestock, were milk, cheese, and yogurt.

The women, or slaves in homes that could afford them, placed these and other foods on big serving trays. They then carried the trays to the dining table. People did not have their own individual plates, but ate food directly from the trays. In addition to milk and water, fruit juices, often mixed with water, were popular. However, wine was uncommon among Abbasid Muslims. This was because Islam banned drinks containing alcohol.

THE PROPHET MUHAMMAD RECOMMENDS MEAT STEW

Evidence shows that Islam's prophet was very fond of a simple dish called *tharid*. It is a meat broth or stew topped by dried breadcrumbs. The prophet Muhammad's likes and dislikes had a strong influence on later Muslims. As a result, *tharid* was widely popular during the Islamic Golden Age.

Religion shaped more than just customs of worship during the Islamic Golden Age. It also affected family life. According to the prophet Muhammad, God wanted society, including families, to be mainly run by men.

Men's and women's roles

In Abbasid times, a husband was the head of a family. He was expected to act responsibly and fulfill certain duties. First, he had to provide a home, food, and clothing for his wife and children. It was also his job to protect them.

By tradition, taking care of the house was a wife's second-most important duty. (The first was having children.) She also had responsibility for raising the children. Women were often so busy with their duties around the house that they rarely left it.

In this illustration, Muhammad and his wife, Aisha, are freeing the daughter of a tribal chief. Tradition says that Muhammad valued his wife's intelligence and listened to her opinions.

Women of child-bearing age were not supposed to mix with men who were not family members. So, on the rare occasions when a woman did go out, she walked with a male relative so that she could be shielded from contact with strange men. During the Golden Age, women and men were expected to stay separated, particularly in public. However, in the poorest city homes, both husbands and wives had to work. So, some poorer men and women worked side by side in marketplaces and shops.

WOMEN'S QUARTERS

An average house had a special room a wife could call her own. There, she might do the sewing or perhaps just rest. It was also the place she and her daughters passed the time when her husband invited men who were not family members into the house.

PICTURES OF MUHAMMAD

Many Muslims believe that artists should not try to draw the prophet Muhammad, as it may lead to people worshiping depictions or statues rather than Muhammad himself. That is why, traditionally, illustrations of the prophet Muhammad often don't show his face. In the illustration opposite, his face is concealed behind a veil. Other illustrations show him wearing very long sleeves to conceal his hands or with a featureless face.

Marriage and divorce

The Islamic religion allowed a husband to have up to four wives at a time. However, he was expected to support each wife equally. That usually meant that he had to maintain a separate household for each, which few could afford to do. As a result, most men had only one wife.

This painted scene from a medieval Turkish book shows Muhammad marrying his first wife, Khadija.

One very important aspect of marriage was a custom called a **dowry**. In the pre-Islamic Middle East, it consisted of money or property the groom gave the bride's father. The bride had a certain value as a laborer in her father's house. The dowry was meant to make up for the father's loss of that value. But after the prophet Muhammad's time, including the Golden Age, the dowry belonged to the bride. Even her husband could not take it from her.

GETTING A DIVORCE

Divorces were fairly common in the Golden Age. Some evidence suggests that all a man had to do was to say aloud three times in a row that he was divorcing his wife. It was much harder for a woman to get a divorce, however. She had to go to court and show good cause. Causes the court might consider included her husband having a terrible disease or if he abandoned her.

A GENEROUS WIFE

A dowry was not the only money that a wife might own and that her husband could not touch. During the Golden Age, women had the right to inherit both money and property. A husband was allowed to use such money only if his wife gave her permission. The prophet Muhammad's first wife, Khadijah, was very wealthy when they married. She chose to allow him to use her money. "When I was poor," he later said, "she shared her wealth with me."

The stages of childhood

During the Golden Age, Muslims recognized four stages of childhood. The first lasted from birth until a child began getting his or her baby teeth. One of the first duties toward children during this stage was to put them on the path to becoming a Muslim. Soon after a baby was born, a parent whispered in its ear the words of the call to prayer. These were the same words the muezzin called out five times each day.

PUPPET THEATERS

Puppet theaters were popular in the early Islamic centuries. Two different types of puppet existed. One was the kind that hung on strings, today called **Marionettes**. The other was hand puppets, usually cloth figures that fit over a person's hand. The people making the puppets move also did their voices.

Childhood's second stage went from teething to the age of 7. The third lasted from the age of 7 to 13 or 14. During these stages, children learned correct manners and social behavior from their parents and other relatives. Some children also started going to school.

Many toys were similar to those that children enjoy today. Girls had dolls, for instance. Both boys and girls liked seesaws and miniature animals made from cloth, leather, or wood.

Young adults

The fourth stage of childhood ended around the age of 15. Before this age, children were not required to do the rituals of the Five Pillars. But as young adults, they were expected to begin doing them regularly. This age was also when young people often started thinking about marriage. The average age that girls got married was their early- to mid-teens. Boys tended to be a bit older—in their late teens or early twenties.

This painting shows wealthy medieval Muslim families preparing for a wedding.

23

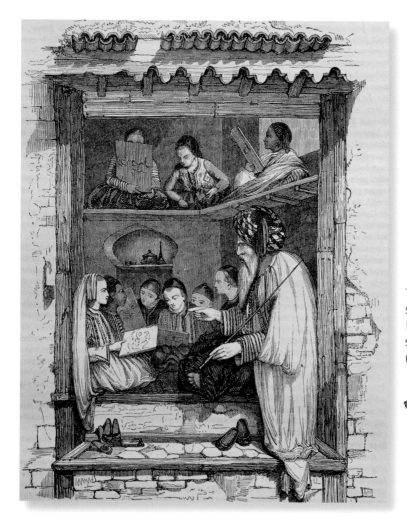

This Muslim schoolmaster in Morocco is teaching schoolgirls how to read the Quran.

During the Islamic Golden Age, boys usually received a better education than girls. This was partly because society thought women should stay at home, so girls did not need to be as well educated as boys. However, both boys and girls were expected to master the Quran.

Schools for boys

Boys from wealthy homes usually received an excellent education, but education was also available to less wealthy boys if they and their parents wanted it.

STUDENTS NEED A BREAK!

Writing in the late Abbasid period, a respected **scholar**, al-Ghazali, said that constant learning without a break was not good for students. He said they should take breaks to play ball games and watch puppet shows.

Most boys went to school in their local mosque. Meanwhile, boys from the richest homes were taught by private tutors, often in those teachers' own homes. In both settings, it was common for the teacher to sit on a mat on the floor, facing toward Mecca. The students sat in a curved line, facing him.

At first, the boys learned to read and write Arabic by studying verses from the Quran. Gradually, they memorized them. They also learned basic arithmetic. The most common writing materials were a wooden board and a pen made from a river reed. A boy dipped the pen in ink made from soot and wrote on the board. When he was finished, he washed off the ink, leaving the board blank for the next lesson.

Students seeking higher education studied Islamic law. And as the Golden Age blossomed in the 800s CE and 900s CE, other areas of learning became popular as well. These included geography and astronomy.

With the rise of learning, the sciences progressed. This is Jabir, a Persian who is widely thought of as the Father of Chemistry. He was also a philosopher and engineer.

Teaching girls

Girls did not usually go to formal schools during the Golden Age. Instead, most of them were taught by their parents at home. The girls learned about Islam's beliefs and customs. At the same time, their mothers taught them how to cook, make clothes, and perform other household duties.

Sometimes, however, young women received educations equal to those of young men. Some wealthy parents, especially fathers who were scholars, chose to educate their daughters beyond the basics of religious studies. Clearly, these men took the prophet Muhammad's earlier praise of female religious scholars seriously. He called the women of the Arabian town of Medina "splendid" for "becoming learned in the faith." Following that example, some young women in the Golden Age attended lectures given to boys in the mosques. Others studied with private tutors paid for by their fathers.

HOW DO WE KNOW?

A girl shows spirit in school

Some older men did not approve of girls attending classes in medieval mosques. One of them wrote, "Women come too, to hear the readings. The men sit in one place, the women facing them." He was shocked at one girl's behavior, which he saw as unruly. He remembered she was rude enough to "stand up [and] shout in a loud voice."

The emphasis on learning led to the rise of universities. This picture shows the entrance to the University of Al-Karaouine in Morocco.

As a result, a few women became scholars and teachers themselves. We know details about this thanks to Ibn Asikir, a traveler and expert on the Quran in late Abbasid times. He visited most of the best schools in the Middle East. He reported that of the teachers he met, 1,300 were men and 80 were women. Some educated women also taught the Quran in houses run by charities for orphans and homeless people.

Although the Muslims of the Golden Age were very religious, they liked to have fun, just as modern people do. They also saw that the Quran did not forbid people from enjoying themselves sometimes. So, whenever they had the time, they took part in a variety of pastimes.

Several games were popular in the Golden Age. This early-modern painting, *The Backgammon Players,* captures that game's popularity.

Theater

Theater with live actors did not yet exist in the Middle East. However, a version called Shadow Theater, featuring some unusual puppets, did. The shows were presented just after sunset in the palaces, on street corners, and elsewhere. Men and women from all social classes eagerly gathered to watch them.

The shadow puppets, designed to look like people and animals, were not marionettes on strings. Rather, they were **two-dimensional**, meaning flat. They were usually about 1 foot (30 centimeters) tall and made of camel hide. The puppeteers made them move by controlling long, thin rods attached to the puppets' arms and legs. A bright lantern cast shadows of the moving puppets onto a large screen made of white cloth. As the audience watched, the dark figures walked, danced, and even fought one another. The puppeteers provided the characters' voices, while musicians played background music.

RELAXING AT THE BATHS

Public baths existed in almost every Abbasid town. Both men and women attended. They either went on different days or used separate bath buildings. These elegant structures often had marble or **mosaic** floors and elaborate decorations. Servants poured hot or cold water over the customers as they lounged in shallow pools of water. Bathers also met with friends and caught up on the latest news. In addition, they could buy snacks or even full meals. However, entry into the bath itself was usually free.

Sports and other contests

A love for contests seems to have been an important part of ancient Arab culture. In the early 800s CE, chess contests called **tournaments** were held. The best players from around the empire took part.

Most sports were dominated by men, but women were allowed to play polo—although only against other women. Other popular sports included archery, wrestling, and all sorts of races.

Polo, like today, involved two teams on horseback using long mallets to hit the ball into a goal.

Hunting

Perhaps the most common of all the leisure pastimes in the Golden Age was hunting. Rich people could afford to organize hunting parties, with hunting dogs and birds to chase down the prey. They could also afford expensive carriages and servants or slaves to carry and place them. For rich people, hunting was mainly about sport. In contrast, poorer people hunted for another reason. They enjoyed it as a sport, but they also did it to get extra food for their families. Their main weapon was the bow and arrow, sometimes aided by an iron-tipped spear.

Hunting was a popular sport, especially among wealthy people. Here, a hunter uses a net to trap some birds.

Some of the animals hunted were mammals such as hares, deer, antelopes, and wild donkeys. Other common animals hunted were birds, including ducks and geese. A few daring hunters even went after fierce lions, which lived in parts of the countryside at the time.

Falconry

Hunts organized by wealthy people included the use of hunting birds. This combined two sports in one. The first, of course, was hunting itself. The second was the very ancient practice of **falconry**. Falcons and hawks are large, lethal, and highly intelligent birds. In the wild, they have a powerful instinct to chase and kill small animals. Training them to do that for human owners is an art that existed in Asia long before the rise of Islam.

The first three Abbasid centuries witnessed major advances in the arts and sciences. In fact, that is the main reason this period is called Islam's Golden Age. Several caliphs encouraged these advances. But it was al-Mamun, who ruled from 813 CE to 833 CE, who was most active and influential in promoting them.

At al-Mamun's request, the leaders of the Greek-speaking Byzantine Empire sent him works by well-known ancient Greek thinkers, including Plato and Aristotle. The caliph hired **translators** to create Arabic versions of these books. Then, Arabic scholars used those works to help advance their own research. The result was a centuries-long period of important achievements in medicine, astronomy, mathematics, architecture, and literature.

HOW WE SEE

Another Muslim scientist helped doctors to better understand how people's eyes work. Born in 965 CE, Ibn al-Hazen discovered that the earlier explanation of "seeing" was wrong. It claimed that people see objects because light moves out of their eyes and touches those objects. Al-Hazen correctly showed that seeing occurs when light reflects off objects and then enters the eyes.

Medical advances

Doctors and medical researchers opened many new clinics and hospitals in Abbasid cities. They tried different healing methods and medicines. As a result, they found hundreds of herbs and drugs that effectively treated common problems such as headaches, stomach pains, and snakebites.

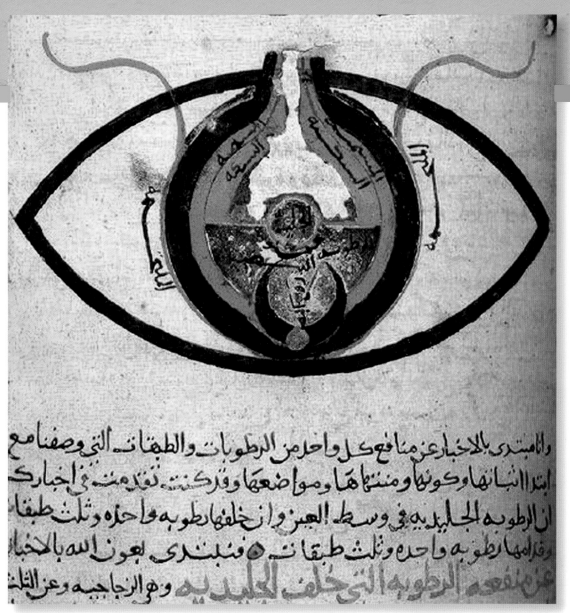

Muslim doctors also developed new surgical tools and methods. In the past, there had been no way to dull the pain caused by cutting people open. So, patients undergoing surgery had to be held down and allowed to scream. Such horrors ended when Golden Age doctors found drugs that made a patient sleep during an operation. They also learned to use animal intestines to make thread for sewing patients up after surgery.

Knowledge about human biology and understanding of organs, such as the eye, increased as the sciences developed.

Other scientific achievements

The impressive work of Muslim doctors was only one of many scientific advances made during the Islamic Golden Age. Thousands of young men pursued careers in several scientific fields. Their efforts made a number of aspects of daily life and work easier.

Some striking advances in mathematics and astronomy are clear examples. One achievement that stood out was the work of a math expert named al-Khwarizmi. He created a new system of numbers that came to be called Arabic numerals and the **decimal system.**

This method, along with other Golden Age math advances, made counting and calculating simpler. For instance, it was far easier for farmers to count the crops they harvested and sold. Merchants and tax collectors were able to keep more precise records. And builders could more exactly measure plots of land and the floor plans of houses.

Al-Khwarizmi created the counting system using Arabic numerals, which we use today.

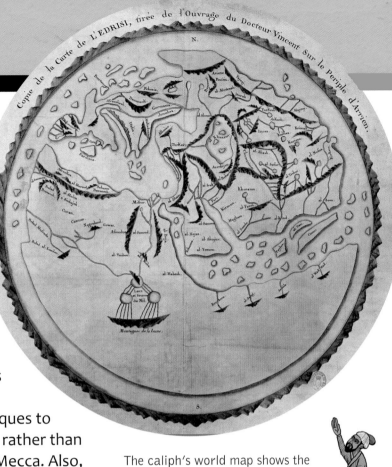

Copie de la Carte de L'EDRISI, tirée de l'Ouvrage du Docteur Vincent sur le Periple d'Arrien.

The new math also helped astronomers and geographers in their work. They used studies of the stars and planets to make more accurate measurements of distances and directions on the Earth's surface. In turn, this allowed builders of mosques to point them in the exact, rather than estimated, direction of Mecca. Also, religious officials could be more exact about the times for daily prayer.

The caliph's world map shows the continents that were known then: Europe (top left), Asia (top right), and Africa (bottom).

HOW DO WE KNOW?

The caliph's world map

Improvements made in math and astronomy during the Golden Age made map-making more precise. The caliph al-Mamun therefore ordered new maps to be made. These greatly aided traders, government messengers, and other travelers. One of the caliph's maps shows the known world of his era. Because it was reprinted in later Muslim books, it has survived. It shows Europe, Asia, and Africa and indicates the location of Mecca.

The arts

During the Golden Age, the decorative arts became more advanced. Ceramics, also called pottery-making, and metalwork, meaning the creation of ornaments made of bronze, gold, and other metals, were popular. **Calligraphy**—making elaborate, beautiful, handwritten lettering—was also common.

A master Muslim potter creates some ceramic pots.

Most of the people who bought these—usually expensive—items were members of the upper classes. But production of those items affected many people. The craftworkers themselves benefited because their work was much in demand. Also, over time, that demand created many openings for **apprentices**. Young people learned a trade by assisting a master craftworker. Eventually, they became masters themselves.

Architecture

Architects designed buildings to be attractive. But those structures also had to be strong and stable. Otherwise, they might crack, sag, or even collapse. Muslim architects and builders developed scientific construction methods that made larger and larger structures possible. As a result, Baghdad and other Abbasid cities featured enormous palaces. There were also huge bathhouses and mosques that held hundreds of people at a time. Many had running water for drinking and bathing, and drains that carried dirty water to sewers beneath the streets.

BURIED WITH A PEN

The beautiful lettering created by Muslim calligraphers decorated all kinds of objects, such as vases, metal swords, and fine fabrics. Calligraphy also decorated the covers and pages of books, including versions of the Quran. An apprentice practiced for many years to become a master of the art. One key to his success was to cut reeds for the tips of his pens in just the right way. Indeed, many calligraphers kept their pens in metal boxes for protection. Some of these artists were buried holding their favorite pen in one hand.

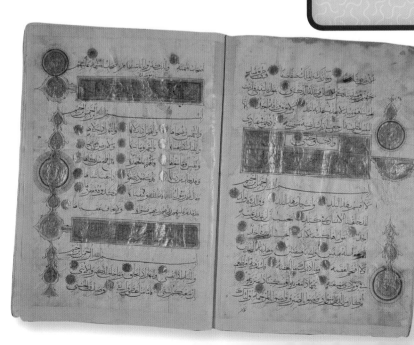

This Turkish version of the Quran features beautiful decorations.

A wealth of stories

Stories about romance and adventure in faraway places became widely popular during the Golden Age. Tales about characters with magical powers, like sorcerers and **genies**, were especially well liked. The best-known example is *The Book of One Thousand and One Nights*, a large collection of folk tales. People also enjoyed poetry and often sang the verses to music.

A giant man-eating bird called the "roc" attacks the ship of the heroic Sinbad the Sailor in this drawing of the popular folk tale.

Poetry and stories were often richly decorated with beautiful illustrations.

During the period, there was a massive rise in **literacy,** the ability to read and write. Almost every member of the Abbasid upper classes was literate. Many ordinary people could also read. Mainly, this was because of the Muslim social tradition that urged many young people to learn to read the Quran.

This expansion of literacy and book publishing had far-reaching effects on society. First, printing presses did not yet exist. So, each book had to be copied by hand, which created full-time work for thousands of people. Also, increasing numbers of people bought and collected books. Poorer people who could not afford to buy them read copies in libraries inside mosques. Caliphs and other wealthy individuals supplied the volumes for those expanding collections. They also gave books to many new libraries built outside the mosques.

Paper мaking

In addition, publishing thousands of books required a lot of paper. Before the Golden Age, paper had been an expensive luxury imported and used mainly by the rich. But Abbasid manufacturers borrowed new paper-making methods from China. This led to a lower-cost type of paper that made book production far cheaper. In turn, as the cost of books decreased, more ordinary people could afford to buy them. As a result, even more people were inspired to learn to read.

In the 1100s and 1200s, parts of Abbasid culture started filtering into Europe. Christians mingled, traded, and exchanged ideas with Muslims in Islamic communities in Spain and on the island of Sicily. As a result, several Christian kings began wearing splendid robes made with Muslim fabrics. European churchmen and craftworkers also adopted styles of Arabic calligraphy. These went on to decorate European palaces, churches, and expensive clothing.

Life in the Islamic Golden Age strongly influenced later generations of both Muslims and non-Muslims. Muslims who lived in the post-Abbasid years could look back with pride. Clearly, their civilization had reached a high level. The fine literature of that age influenced Muslim writers of early modern times. Similarly, styles of Islamic architecture created during the Golden Age have lasted well. Modern architects and builders of mosques and other Muslim structures also still use some of them.

Modern mosques, such as this one in Abu Dhabi, still use styles of architecture made popular in the Golden Age.

Islamic art continues to influence decoration and architecture throughout the world.

As time went on, Europe experienced more and more Arabic and Islamic influences. Several European scholars learned Arabic and translated the Arabic versions of ancient Greek texts into Latin. They also translated some of the scientific works of Golden Age Muslim scholars. This information contributed to the emergence of Europe's Renaissance. That period, lasting from the 1300s through to the 1500s, witnessed important advances in art, science, and other cultural areas. These advances were so great that the end of the Renaissance merged with the start of the modern era. In these ways, the Islamic Golden Age played a significant role in the shaping of today's world.

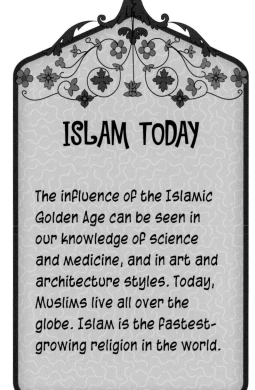

ISLAM TODAY

The influence of the Islamic Golden Age can be seen in our knowledge of science and medicine, and in art and architecture styles. Today, Muslims live all over the globe. Islam is the fastest-growing religion in the world.

A Day in the Life of a Child in the Islamic Golden Age

My name is Zara and I live in a large house on the outskirts of Baghdad. I am 12 years old. Every morning I rise from my bed that I share with my two younger sisters. We take out our prayer mats and pray for the first time.

After prayer, we help our mother and our slave prepare breakfast of bread and fruit in the courtyard of our house. We carry it on a large platter to the dining room, where my father and older brother sit at a large table.

We eat together, and then my father leaves for work. My brother sets off to the mosque, where he goes to school. I wish I could go. He is learning about arithmetic and literature.

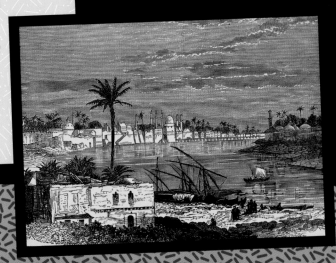

Mother says I should stay at home and learn how to run a household. She is teaching me to make clothes. My older sister married last year and is now busy with her baby and caring for her husband's family. My father has a husband in mind for me. I'll be married in two years.

In the afternoon, I go with my grandfather into town. We visit the market, where we buy fish and fruit. It is a bustling place and I like to see the sights and take in all the different smells of food and spices

When I return, I do the household chores while my mother makes us fish stew for dinner. My favorite! My father and brother return home, and we eat together.

My parents are going out tonight. I light an oil lamp and play chess with my brother until bedtime. I am determined to beat him one day!

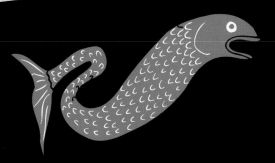

384 BCE
The Greek scholar and thinker Aristotle, who will later have a strong influence on Muslim scholars, is born

570 CE
Islam's final prophet, Muhammad, is born in Mecca, in western Arabia

610 CE
According to the prophet Muhammad, he received his first visit from the angel Gabriel, who informed him that he, the prophet Muhammad, was God's prophet

629 CE
The prophet Muhammad and his followers come to power in Mecca

632 CE
The prophet Muhammad dies at the age of 63

636 CE
An Arab Muslim army defeats a military force of the powerful Byzantine Empire, centered on the Black Sea

640 CE
Muslims change the direction they pray from towards Jerusalem to towards Mecca

661-750 CE
The Umayyad caliphs rule the expanding Islamic Empire

711 CE
A Muslim army crosses the Strait of Gibraltar and enters southern Spain

732 CE
Frankish general Charles Martel defeats a Muslim army at Tours (or Poitiers), in France, halting further Muslim movement into Europe

750 CE
The Umayyad **dynasty** ends, and the first Abbasid ruler takes the throne. Modern experts mark this date as the start of the Islamic Golden Age.

762 CE
The Abbasids build a new city—Baghdad, in what is now Iraq—to become their capital

813–833 CE
These years mark the reign of the Abbasid caliph al-Mamun, who strongly promotes the arts and sciences

836 CE
The Abbasids move their capital to Samarra, about 100 miles (160 kilometers) north of Baghdad

892 CE
The capital moves once again to Baghdad

1099 CE
European Crusaders capture Jerusalem, then in Muslim territory

c. 1100s AND 1200s CE
Muslim writings and ideas begin entering Europe

1220 CE
Mongol armies begin invading Muslim lands in southwestern Asia

1258 CE
The Mongols capture Baghdad, ending the Abbasid dynasty

Allah the name Muslims use for God

apprentice person who trains under an expert in a craft, trade, or profession

BCE short for "Before the Common Era," relating to dates before the birth of Jesus Christ

caliph ruler of a Muslim nation or empire during medieval times

calligraphy art of making elaborate, beautiful, handwritten lettering

CE short for "Common Era," relating to dates after the birth of Jesus Christ

convert change from following one religion to another

decimal system mathematical system based on multiples of 10

dowry money or property brought by a woman to her husband at marriage

dynasty family line of rulers

excavation digging up the remains of past civilizations

falconry sport in which a hunter uses a trained falcon or other bird of prey to hunt or perform other feats

genie supernatural or magical creature mentioned often in Arabic and Islamic stories and writings

Hajj pilgrimage to Mecca. All Muslims are expected to make the journey at least once during their life if they can afford it.

Islam religion started by the prophet Muhammad in the early 600s CE

literacy reading and writing

marionette puppet that hangs from strings

Middle East region along the southeastern border of the Mediterranean Sea, from Libya in North Africa to Afghanistan in Asia

mosaic picture made up of thousands of small tiles, stones, shells, or pieces of glass

Muslim follower of the Islamic religion

nomad person who has no permanent home and moves often from place to place

pilgrimage journey made for religious reasons

prophet person chosen by a god to be his or her messenger on Earth

ritual set way of going through the steps of a religious ceremony

scholar person who has studied and gained knowledge

tournament large-scale contest held in public

translator person who changes words from one language into another

two-dimensional flat

Books

Guillain, Charlotte. *Islamic Culture* (Global Cultures). Chicago: Heinemann Library, 2013.

Meredith, Susan, and Clare Hickman. *The Usborne Encyclopedia of World Religions*. Tulsa, Okla.: EDC, 2010.

Toor, Atif. *Islamic Culture* (Discovering the Arts). Vero Beach, Fla.: Rourke, 2006.

Wallace, Holly. *Islam* (Our World of Faith). Mankato, Minn.: New Forest, 2012.

Web sites

Facthound offers a safe, fun way to find internet sites related to this book. All of the sites have been researched by our staff.

Here's all you do:
Visit www.facthound.com
Type in this code: 9781484608319

Places to visit

Visiting the Middle East, especially Iraq or Egypt, would be the ideal way to learn about early Islam and the history of Islamic art. However, many fascinating collections of Arabic and Islamic objects and exhibits can be seen at museums.

The Freer and Sackler Galleries, Washington, D.C.
www.asia.si.edu
The Freer and Sackler Galleries have some of the most impressive examples of Islamic art in the United States.

The Metropolitan Museum of Art, New York
www.metmuseum.org
Visit the Metropolitan Museum of Art to see many objects from the Middle East.

How can I find out more?

One good way to find out more about the Islamic Golden Age is by taking online walking tours. These are web sites that lead visitors from one page to another, showing photos of cities in the Middle East and elsewhere and the Islamic arts they contain. One of the best of these sites is called "Islamic Arts and Architecture."

INDEX